MW00440826

LIVE HANDS

A KEY
TO
BETTER GOLF

BY
ERIC PRAIN

NEW FOREWORD BY
W. TIMOTHY GALLWEY

WITH AN INTRODUCTION BY
BERNARD DARWIN

WARDE PUBLISHERS
PORTOLA VALLEY, CALIFORNIA

Live Hands was first published in 1946 by A & C Black (Publishers) Ltd., London England

The book is being reprinted in the United States, Canada and other territories by Warde Publishers, Inc. under license from A & C Black. All rights reserved. No part of this publication may be reproduced, stored in a retrieval system, or transmitted, in any form or by any means, electronic, photocopying, recording, or otherwise without the prior written permission of the publisher, except in the case of brief excerpts in critical reviews and articles. For permission requests, write to the publisher, addressed "Attention: Permission" at the address below:

Warde Publishers, Inc.
3000 Alpine Rd.
Portola Valley, CA 94028
1-800-699-2733

Warde Publishers wishes to acknowledge the contribution of Mr. Robert Brue, a Senior PGA Tour Member, who brought this book to our attention.

Cataloging-in-Publication Data

Prain, E. M. (Eric M.)
    Live hands : a key to better golf / by E. M. Prain ; with a new foreword by W. Timothy Gallwey ; introduction by Bernard Darwin. — 1st ed.
    p.   cm.
    1. Golf   I. Title
GV965.P7 1998   796.352
                                              QBI97–41581

Printed in the United States of America

10 9 8 7 6 5 4 3 2 1   99 98

Cover Design: The Design Den

Text Design: Penna Design

Publisher's Note: Prior to publication of this reprint of
Live Hands, *we interviewed Eric Prain by telephone from his home in London, England. We hope the following biographical information provides insight into how Mr. Prain came to write this entertaining and instructional golf book.*

Eric Prain was born in Dundee, Scotland in 1908.
In 1909, the Prain family moved to St. Andrews, Scotland. Eric attended the Charterhouse School in England, and in 1927 he entered Cambridge University, and was a member of the Cambridge golf team. Mr. Prain became a member of the Royal and Ancient Golf Club of St. Andrews in 1927.

He was also a member of the famous team which won the prestigious Halford Hewitt Cup a record eight times in eleven years. As an amateur golfer he competed with many well known British stars of the day such as Raymond Oppenheimer. In 1930 and 1936, he was named by Oppenheimer to the British teams which competed against France.

In 1933, Mr. Prain began a lifelong career in journalism, working initially for the London office of *Time* Magazine. During this pre-war period and after the war he was the golf writer for three major British newspapers including the *Guardian*, *The Sunday Express*, and *The Evening Standard*. Mr. Prain's career in journalism was highlighted by his appointment to the position of Leader Writer for *The*

Evening Standard, a position reserved for the most respected journalists in the country.

In 1939, Eric Prain joined the Rifle Brigade of the British Army and during the war years he served in North Africa.

Mr. Prain wrote *Live Hands* in a four-month period immediately following the war; the book was originally published in 1946.

Mr. Prain worked as a journalist until his retirement in 1953. He is also an accomplished landscape and seascape painter. His works have been exhibited by the Royal Society of British Artists and the Chenil Galleries in Chelsea.

January 1998

C O N T E N T S

ILLUSTRATIONS

FOREWORD

BY W. TIMOTHY GALLWEY

*E*ric Prain's *Live Hands*, written over fifty years ago, represents eloquently the golfer's quest for the secret formula to the game. Even those years before the advent of video and the explosion of modern golfing techniques the golfer seemed to have been beset by the complexity of those who would analyze and dictate the proper and sequential movement of hips, forearms, shoulders, feet, etc.

Prain's instincts were good. Cut through the complexity at any price. Find the simplicity. If you don't, golf will continue to be a series of exalted hopes followed by dashed dreams.

In the Forties, this must have been a bold statement. Even in the Nineties, to affirm simplicity takes a conviction born only from practice and profound experience. It was in the hands and their living connection with the club that Prain found the simplicity of the golf swing, from putting to driving and everything in between.

Realizing that golf is a game of controlling many moving parts in exacting rhythm and timing, he writes, "let the hands control." This is the mantra of this marvelously written little book.

But not just *let the hands control,* let the hands live, let them be alive to the presence of the club head — the only moving part that makes contact with the all too still and silent ball.

It is in his effort to articulate a "living" relationship between hands and club that Prain becomes a true prophet of things to come. If all he had to say was that the hands should lead the rest of the body in the golf swing, he would be in the company of the many who have selected one of the many components of the golf swing to be the master element of the rest. For example, there are those who say that if you simply grip the club correctly and assume the right posture at the outset, all else will follow naturally. Others counsel that the proper rotation of the hips and shoulders, the large muscles, should lead all other movements in the swing. Although Prain might seem to be promoting the "Excalibur" of the dominance of the hands, I don't believe that is the greatest contribution of this book to the art of golf.

The primary reason Prain settles on the hands is that they "are the only part of the player in direct contact with the club." Contact with the club is the thing — but not just physical contact — living contact. The hands, especially the thumb and forefingers of each hand, must feel the clubhead from the waggle before the swing to its final resting place. It is the emphasis on living/feeling — doing whatever you need to do in order to develop a greater feel for what's happening with the clubhead — that Prain takes the bolder step towards the synthesis of mind and body in the golf swing. To speak of the "spark" that must jump between hands and clubhead is to speak about a dimension of golf that few have the courage to write about, but most who play the game know is real.

The game of golf, at its best, is simple because human beings, at their best, are simple. Yet there is a part of each of us that doesn't appreciate that fact. We associate complexity with maturity, sophistication, and knowledge. We assume that to be simple is to be simple-minded. Yet this is not true. Prain's simplicity has been wrought in the fires of the study of golf theory and performance. He has clearly paid his dues, has entered the door of complexity (at least as it existed in the Forties) and emerged a scratch golfer on the other side. The trip is never an easy one, and its destination can easily be missed — by settling on reductionism of one kind or another — a single slogan or tip. But Prain lifts the reader beyond the realm of true feeling.

As the first chapter so eloquently expresses, true simplicity does not exist in formulas, but as a fact of life. The simplicity of breath itself is such a fact. The awareness that allows the eyes to see and the hands to feel is simple (even though what is seen and felt can be construed as almost infinitely complex.) It is our connection with the basic simplicity of our nature that allows us not to be subjugated by the otherwise seeming complexity of things. Then the sparks of life jump from the hands of the club, or to the racquet or to another human hand, the complexity tamed.

Live Hands is about the golf swing, but as all classics on any specific subject, it is a rich lesson on how to approach all things.

INTRODUCTION

$\mathcal{M}$r. Eric Prain has asked me to be a curtain-raiser and I am very glad to do so, both because his book has interested me very much and because he is an old friend. I first met him when he came up to Cambridge as a freshman to join in the always laudable work of trying to beat Oxford. Later I have known him as one of a famous team of Old Carthusians who constantly won the Halford Hewitt Cup at Deal and added to the gaiety of golfers in doing so. I have always thought of him, not only as a very good player, but as one having a singularly easy, graceful and natural style. It comes as a complete surprise to read that he endured such agonies of theorising before he settled down to the simplification of his creed. I can only say that no one would "know it on him." However, these past sufferings of his make all the more valuable his present confession of a simplified faith, in which all such tiresome things as hips and shoulders and knees appear only as the followers—sometimes, as we all know, the very unruly followers—of the vital and dominant hands.

I must not steal Mr. Prain's thunder, but I cannot refrain from quoting one sentence of his which seems to me particularly commendable. Of the players in the Open Championship he writes: "It seemed that they had stayed behind the ball until after it was hit, and that the whole weight of the body flowed in behind the shot." That is well said. We have all felt at times that we could play so much better if only we had astral bodies that did not get in the way. He finds in concentration on the work of the hands a way of keeping those "too, too solid" bodies in subjection. This is the truth which he sings "To one clear harp in divers tones."

But though he sings it often, his song does not, if I may respectfully say so, grow monotonous; the best compliment I can pay him is to say that I am almost glad that owing to bodily infirmities I can scarcely play golf any longer. If I could, so persuasive and exciting is he that I should certainly rush out on to the links and indulge in an orgy of practicing and come in several hours later, a physical wreck and having lost most of my few remaining golf balls. It may seem a double-edged compliment but I mean it as a most sincere one, and with that I step aside and entrust the reader to Mr. Prain's entertaining hands.

Bernard Darwin

I

SEARCHING FOR A FORMULA

*A*s his ball sped into the bushes the length of a cricket pitch away, following a disastrous shot with a No. 5, I heard a friend of mine mutter, "I cannot think why I play this beastly cold-blooded game." And then in the heat of the moment he threw the offending club from him. As it flew through the air, straight up the fairway, and making in the direction of the green with an ominous swishing noise, his rage gave way to pleasure. "There," he said, pointing proudly as the club finished close to the flag, "I knew I had it in me: what length! what direction! what accuracy! and with just that suspicion of draw."

It is in moments of extreme indignity that we sometimes speak real truths. Of course, golf is not beastly, but it is a cold-blooded game and it gives us

PLATE I

THE GRIP AND THE STANCE

George Duncan, the player in this photograph, is about to start the back swing. Note the perfect overlapping grip. The hands fit the club as if they had been designed especially for it. They form two Vs on the shaft, and those manipulative fingers, the forefinger and thumb of each hand, are squeezing the sides of the shaft, feeling for the clubhead. Already the hands have assumed control.

Note also the easy stance: the player gives an impression of relaxation. There is a total absence of tension. The knees are slightly flexed, and the feet are comfortably placed.

the time to think. In other ball games, with the sole exception of billiards, things happen so rapidly that we have to make up our mind and execute the stroke in that split second when the ball is coming toward us. There is no time for the intrusion of outside thoughts. Our mind tells us the stroke to play and our muscles obey the mind; the stroke has been played almost before we know it. As time goes on the heat generated by the body relaxes the muscles and we play more naturally than ever. Whether we are playing well or badly, our mind is fresh and our muscles have warmed to their work. We are not worrying how we do it. We are just getting on with the job. As my angry friend said, golf is very cold-blooded. I have often wondered whether so much theory would have been written about it had it been a much faster game. Its very slowness leads to analysis, and furthermore to self-analysis of a kind which is often muddling. The ball, if the truth be known, plays a brilliant defensive game. Confident in its own emplacements, it does nothing to interfere, but waits for the player to attack.

Consider the matter a moment in a mood of exaggeration. The course is empty and you are without a partner. You and the ball are about to start that intimate personal duel in which only one can survive. You know you must attack and you are wondering about your plan. The ball is perfectly calm and brilliantly on the defensive.

You tee up and grasp the club, perhaps a little quickly, and with a number of plans in your mind. You start the address, that preliminary reconnaissance, the probing of the enemy line. Then you launch the assault, trying to stick to one plan, but half-way up the backswing you decide that the time is not ripe.

You drop the club and light a cigarette, and you give the enemy a threatening look while trying to conceal your fear. You walk away and take in the surrounding view. Everything is very peaceful. Some cows are grazing quietly in the field to the right of the tee. A shot landing in that field will hardly disturb their peace, but you know that it will disturb you because it will cost you a stroke.

Trying to eradicate such thoughts you turn again to the tee, eagerly hoping that perhaps you can see a gap in the defenses. Everything is just as it was. The ball is impregnably calm, awaiting the expected attack. You walk to the start line once

PLATE II

THE TOP OF THE BACKSWING

George Duncan is beautifully poised at the top of the backswing. Notice the hands. They are still firmly in control, knowing precisely the present position of the clubhead. Under the direction of the hands, the hips and shoulders have turned, and the full power of the body is concentrated ready to be applied as required by the hands.

more, muttering as you go, "I wonder who it was who said that this is a cold-blooded business."

Only good generals survive. They survive and are successful because experience has taught them the principles and technique of their art. These principles are the basis of their plan, and when they have decided just how they will attack—or the shot they wish to play—they waste no time in attacking, confident of success because they are obeying those principles which have stood the test of time.

These are the good players, the players who know what they want to do and how they are going to do it. To the unpracticed eye the methods they adopt may look somewhat dissimilar, but the good results they obtain are the direct outcome of an individual approach purposely based on old and accepted fundamentals.

The trouble with the rest of us is that we are always groping. We cannot grow as we should like because we have not roots. We are the earth's most changeable disciples, ever ready to try some new tag in the hope it will prove our salvation, equally ready to desert it for another if it does not give us what we want.

In my Cambridge days, besides playing a

plethora of golf, I made a deep study of the theory of the game. I read most of the standard works, and I had, of course, ample opportunity to put these theories into practice. I do not think it an over-statement to say that I ran the whole gamut of theory. I can still recall, in some degree, my mental attitude to the game at that time. I do not know how many times I felt I had found Excalibur. One day my salvation lay in the movement of my hip, the next in the way my shoulder turned, and again I felt I had found it when I opened my somewhat closed stance.

Looking back on it now I know I should have played better had I made the best of my obvious limitations. Instead of wallowing in a mass of theory I should have employed a merciless sifter. I should have been quicker to see how little was really important. I found the meat in the end, but it took me too long to discard the fat and the stuffing. I make these personal observations only because I know the hopeless feeling which assails the changeable disciple. How fleeting are the moments of success and how often the new half-built castle tumbles about him in ruins!

After the spacious Varsity days I became a

PLATE III

HALF-WAY POINT ON

THE DOWNSWING

Arthur Havers is taken at the half-way point on the downswing. The hands are about to turn inwards and bring the clubhead to the ball. By virtue of their unquestioned control the body is severely disciplined. The right side is beginning to move into the stroke, but its activities are governed by the alliance of the hands and clubhead.

spasmodic week-end golfer. I played mainly with friends, many of whom were in the higher handicap grades. It was then I began to realise how large was the world of theorists and how great was their self-castigation. I noticed that many of my friends arrived at the club house intent upon enjoying their game, but as soon as the game had started they played as if under a cloud. They were often rather worried and in some cases frustrated and miserable.

I soon discovered the reason. In the course of one swing they were trying to do six or seven different things. But all that they achieved was an exaggeration of certain actions of that swing which deprived the whole of rhythm. Their minds were focussed on these motions instead of on the ball at their feet. They had forgotten the first principle in golf, which is to hit the ball. Their play was unduly slow and they made a business of pleasure, while their game, far from improving, took a sharp turn for the worse.

As I have already said, around the apron strings of golf there hangs a mass of theory, some of it good in its way, but much of it very confusing. The more we think of this point or that, the more we vacillate. Somehow we must get down to the meat and discard the fat and the stuffing. It is true that for those who have the leisure and patience to do it, this separating process yields much valuable knowledge; since it is only by trial and error that we can learn for ourselves what is unessential, and then, with the courage of conviction, rebuild on what we know to be a sound and practical basis.

The week-end golfer, however, is hardly in this position. He has to earn his living and he has neither the time nor the opportunity to make radical changes in his game. For radical changes cannot be made in the course of eighteen holes. If, in the course of a round, such changes are attempted, they lead at once to a state of mental confusion the same as I noticed in many of my friends, and to which I have referred before. A successful change of style takes much time and hard work. It can only be accomplished over a period under the guidance of the local professional, or through frequent visits to some quiet corner of the course in the company of a bucket of balls. When playing a game—be it only a friendly one—the enjoyment is increased and the results are better if we concentrate on one thing only, namely to hit the ball.

As in other things, so in golf: we must be content to make the best of what we have. We are either too old, or too wicked, to relinquish the habits of years. We have formed our style and we have not the urge or the time to make extensive alterations in it. In using to the best advantage the mould we have already fashioned lies our best chance of enjoying the game and of achieving results in keeping with our merits.

What then are we to do with this unwieldy mass of theory? Clearly we must swallow it in a severely tabloid form. We must extract from it only the vitamins, leaving the bulk to others with more time and better digestions. A process of compression is required whereby all the by-products are eliminated until we are left in the end with the highly concentrated nourishment.

The object of the ensuing chapters is to show in some detail what, in my view, remains when this process of compression is complete, leaving only in the heated crucible the ingredients of a practical formulas which can be applied in all circumstances. It does not claim to be an easy and sure road to scratch, like the correspondence course I once saw advertised, which invited the reader to attain such a handicap by means of six simple lessons. Instead, it aims at improving the present results of the week-end golfer in the higher handicap grades by an easily remembered means which can be applied to his game with the minimum of mental effort. Consciously applied at first, it will soon become a habit.

II

THE ALLIANCE OF HANDS AND CLUBHEAD

*I*f you were to ask a man with an unpracticed eye what impressed him most while watching an Open Championship, he would probably say that it was the ease with which the players executed each shot. The whole thing appeared so effortless and easy that it was annoying to admit that one could not play just as well oneself. No one motion or mannerism, common to them all, stood out so clearly that one could say with certainty that there lay the secret of good golf. All he would do would be to sum up the spectacle broadly, remarking that each swing had polish, a combination of control, balance and timing.

This broad observation would be true, but he would have missed the secret by which these players attain such outstanding ease. It would be correct to say that they did not all stand alike to the ball, that some swung flay and others upright, that some swings were short and others long, but the more practiced eye would notice one point common to them all.

Their hands controlled the club throughout, and they hit the ball with their hands.

The class player gives an impression which I can only describe as "live-handed." His hands are always doing something. They dominate the swing to such an extent that no other movement in it stands out for all to see. It is this factor which produces a spectacle of smooth and rhythmic ease. It is this factor, too, the control of the club by the hands and the hitting of the ball with the hands through the medium of the clubhead, which makes the first-class golfer. It is, in fact, the Excalibur which raises him out of the ruck. It is the secret of good golf, and of better golf by the week-end golfer.

The importance of the hands is not a discovery. It is as old as the game itself. In doctrines about the game, both written and verbal, it has often been mentioned before. But I think it has been content to lie modestly submerged, depressed by a lot of theory about hips, shoulders and pivots, there to be discovered by those who delved, but eluding the less persistent. It is time it came to the surface.

If we are honest with ourselves we know that, as week-end golfers, we are far too prone to make too much use of the body. We suffer, if you like, from too much body urge. How often have we said—after a particularly disastrous shot—that we hit the ball with the stomach? This is not so much a metaphor as we should like to believe. The phrase carries this much truth, the body has got there first. It has got there first because we have failed to allow the hands to control the clubhead. In the course of the swing we have lost the feeling of that particular part of the club with which, after all, we were designed to hit the ball. With nothing left to hit with, at some point in the swing the body has decided to take control. With nothing to offer instead, and desiring to remove the ball from its present position by means either fair or foul, we permit the eager body to proceed with results which we know so well.

This struggle between the body and the hands

PLATE IV

THE MOMENT OF IMPACT

Craig Wood taken at the moment of impact: the hands are still dictating. They are saying to the body: "Stay where you are. We'll tell you when we want you." By reason of their mastery the player's weight is coming in behind the shot. Although the clubhead is now travelling at maximum speed, its speed is still controlled. The body is balanced and ready, awaiting the word from the hands.

never ceases in the average golfer. The pity is that the body invariably wins. I am sure that it wins only because we have not realised the importance of swinging the clubhead with the hands, and of making sure that the hands hit the ball through the medium of the clubhead. If we are thinking golfers at all, we are so obsessed with some movement or other in the swing that we focus our concentration on it instead of devoting our mental energies to feeling and swinging the clubhead. The hands are dead; the body is too much alive.

As the hands are the only part of the player in direct contact with the club, it is only right and logical that they should be in control. They are invested with that sense of timing without which all is lost. We all know that in order to deliver a blow the clubhead must describe an arc. Obviously it cannot do this of its own accord. It must be guided by some other influence, and an influence intimately connected with it. Clearly the hands are that influence. We must use them; they must navigate throughout. If you are doubtful of the importance of the hands, try this experiment for yourself. Tee up a ball and, standing with the feet together, hit it as hard as you can using the hands and wrists. You will find that the body turn is minimised by the fact that the feet are locked. There will, of course, be a slight turning of the shoulders and hips which will come to pass in a natural manner, since, by reason of the locking of the feet, there is no other means of swinging the club except by the hands and wrists. It is just such a feeling that we wish to engender. Avoid, as far as possible, any lifting of the body as you take the club back. If you really use the hands this lifting will not take place. There will be a slight feeling of impotence, due to the shutting of the feet, but take your courage in both hands and hit the ball with them. I think you will be surprised at the distance and direction obtained. "When you get married," it is often said, "begin as you mean to carry on." In golf this is sage advice. Get away to a good start and you greatly improve your chances of finishing in control. The hands must be given the chance to set the clubhead in motion.

But their purpose does not end there, they must retain that feeling of the clubhead throughout the stroke. The clubhead must be an animate thing living in the hands. It must not become supine or dead. This is the very feeling that subjugates the

PLATE V

AFTER IMPACT

Bobby Locke taken just after the moment of impact: it is obvious from this photograph that the hands and clubhead have worked in unison. Together they are following the ball, now on its way to the green. Note how the right side, when properly controlled, comes in easily behind the shot. All the spectators, but one, are looking to see what has happened. That one, a more discerning gentleman, is looking to see how it happened. Is he watching Locke's hands?

body, an offending bulk which, if it is not properly controlled, will interfere just when it is least required.

The trouble with most of us is that we put the cart before the horse. We look upon the golf swing as a series of movements made by various parts of the body whose sum total will eventually bring the clubhead to the ball. In a golf stroke properly executed, it is the hands which bring the clubhead to the ball, and the various antics which the body and feet perform are dictated by the hands in the journey they make through the arc of the golf swing. If the hands are in control those movements we worry so much about are resolved in a natural manner.

So far as the golf swing is concerned, in order to keep any part of it in perspective we must review the action as a whole. For it is at its best an unbroken motion. To stress one part unduly must destroy the rhythmic flow. There is a time and a place for each movement, and none should be consciously forced into place until the timing of the machine is ready to receive it. Each will fit in a natural manner when it is really required.

No venture can be successful unless someone is in control. It will not do if the various members dash here and there, accomplishing this and that on their own account without regard to the doings of others, uncertain if their efforts have a direct bearing on the object, not knowing if they are being duplicated in some other quarter. There must be a master unit which directs, plans and controls. The golf swing is a rhythmic motion, and every rhythmic motion has a guiding, controlling force.

When we swing a golf club, what exactly is our object? Our object is to hit the ball with the clubhead attaining at the same time the maximum speed and accuracy at the moment of impact. We cannot achieve our object unless we have some form of control. To function efficiently, that control must be vested in something with an intimate connection with the clubhead. The hands are the only part of the body in direct contact with the club. Clearly they must control.

The spectator at the Open Championship, in his broad summary of what he saw, remarked that control was a feature of all the players. They gave a decided impression of playing within themselves. It appeared that they had a carefully husbanded reserve ready to be used whenever it was wanted. This impression was created because, through the feel of it in their hands, they swung the clubhead and brought it to the ball with the maximum speed and accuracy at the moment of impact. It seemed that they had stayed behind the ball until after it was hit and that the whole weight of the body flowed in behind the shot.

In other words, they hit the ball with the hands through the medium of the clubhead.

The movements of each player's body were perfectly synchronised. It was all so smooth that you could not detect one motion from another. This pleasing camouflage was achieved because all these movements were controlled. The whole performance looked natural because, through that intimate feeling between the hands and the clubhead, and not through any conscious thought on the part of the player, these movements fitted easily into place. They appeared, functioned and faded without disturbing the rhythmic flow, since they were not forced or studied. They remained natural since they could not do other than they did. Controlled by the hands they are natural movements and follow as night follows day. Really they are not our worry.

Some years ago, in America, I was discussing

golf with Johnny Anderson, who was at that time Olympic discus champion. Johnny was a good golfer and a student of the game. He told me then that the function of the hand was no less important in discus throwing. He explained that when his body preceded his hand at the moment of the throw, the length and direction suffered. The discus flew off to the right and the throw was some feet short of normal. But if the hand came through first, pulling the weight of the body behind it, the throw was both long and straight.

The analogy to golf is exact. The hand in each case provides the motive force, directly in discus throwing, and indirectly in golf through the medium of the clubhead. Hand control ensures that the full weight of the body is massed behind the shot and applied in its proper place. Balance was mentioned as another quality common to all good players. How then do we achieve it? If balance was not natural in everyone they could not stand comfortably in a room nor could they walk down the street. The first is balance in a static condition; the second is balance in motion. We are apt to think of balance as something to be consciously attained, perhaps by a studied transfer of weight from one direction to another. If left to its own devices balance will look after itself, for it is a gift natural to everyone. It is born in us. The good golfer achieves it because he is content to let it function naturally. If all movements of the golf swing are synchronised by means of a supreme control, balance is bound to follow.

Sometimes I have heard the remark, "I shall never improve at this game. You see, I have no sense of timing." What then is timing? Applied to golf, one definition might be that timing is the co-ordination of mind and muscle which brings the clubhead to the ball with the maximum speed at the moment of impact. Yet the same people who doubt that this valuable sense is in them have no difficulty in knocking a nail into a piece of wood with a hammer. Perhaps they have not looked at it in this light, but such a task requires a sense of timing. If they can do this, and anyone can, though some are more skilled than others, then the sense is there alright; it needs to be developed.

Compared to a golf club a hammer lacks balance. The golf club is a more sensitive instrument. The head of the hammer is heavily weighted and there is no mistaking its presence. But the golf club has a finer balance with the feel of the head less pronounced and unless we are alive to its significance we lose the most valuable adjunct in helping us to play well. So much mental energy is wasted thinking about hips, shoulders, the left arm or the right elbow, all of which will look after themselves provided they are controlled by that close relationship between the hands and the clubhead. The closer the relationship which exists between these two the better the sense of timing. Anyone can improve their timing and, *ipso facto,* their golf by a studied effort to encourage this bond.

The other day I played a few holes with a member of the local club. I had not played with him before and I think his handicap was six. He had an ungainly style and an upright swing, and I was amazed how consistently he hit the ball down the middle of the fairway. The ball flew from the club with a sweet, mellow crack. Interested by results from methods so seemingly unpolished I watched carefully for the reason. I found the answer in the hands. The shoulders and hips moved the bare minimum and the face of the club was shut throughout. It seemed at first sight that the result should have been a hook or a smothered shot. But the player's hands saved him. From start to finish of the swing they were firmly in control, swinging the clubhead and bringing it through to the ball.

I found that in the course of his work he used his hands a great deal. I believe his "live-handedness" was brought about by an unconscious effort on his part. They were strong, and it was natural for him to use them. I do not believe the player knew to what he owed his success.

It is a pity that as we grow older we lose that youthful gift, the faculty for imitation. Young boys and girls who start the game early acquire a natural swing by watching and imitating some good player. Many have a very fine swing without ever having a lesson. Many also can give a truly life-like imitation of the eccentric methods of players they have seen. If the youthful eye is quick to grasp the right way to swing, it has also an unerring capacity to reproduce something unusual.

I remember how proud I was as a boy of a reproduction I often gave of a player I once saw at St. Andrews. With the precociousness of youth, I used to delight in the amusement this imitation gave to grown-ups.

This man was standing on the sixth tee of the

Eden Course. The hole runs parallel to the shore of the estuary of the river Eden. Since the fifth green is so close to the sixth tee, it is both a safety precaution and a matter of common courtesy not to play to the green until the players in front are off the tee. Another small boy and I were patiently waiting to approach the green as we watched this gentleman tee up.

He began with a series of ungainly and vicious waggles which increased in fury, if not in beauty, until he had made nearly fifty. At last his clubhead came to rest behind the ball. It would soon be over, we thought. But not at all. He remained there, rigid and immobile, a fixture in the peaceful landscape, in an effort, one assumed, to hypnotise the ball to yield to his will. Nothing broke the silence save the lapping of the waves on the shore. I looked at my watch and I timed him. For a minute or more nothing happened. I had the urge to laugh. One felt that tense expectancy which sometimes assails one when waiting for an explosion. Just when it was least expected, and as if a button had been pressed, everything happened at once. A mighty heave of the body synchronised with a wicked lunge. The performance was over in a flash and his swing—if you can call it such—was the shortest I have ever seen. Needless to say he was playing by himself for no one could have stood that for a round. We passed through him soon afterwards still searching for his ball on the beach. His performance, of course, was easy to imitate and I believe I could still do it now. Perhaps he was a hypnotist on holiday who had played much hockey in his youth.

One day shortly before the war I was playing golf with a friend at a well-known course where Mr. X was the equally well-known professional. Mr. X was a famous stylist. We had finished our round and we made our way towards the caddy-master's shed to pay off our caddies. While waiting for some change I happened to glance out of the window, and I saw in a rough patch of grass at the back of the shed a small boy swinging an old and rusty iron. That boy had a lovely swing. I collected my change and went straight out of the shed towards that patch of grass. The small boy continued time after time to swing the club with a beautiful ease.

"Who taught you to swing like that?" I said.

The boy looked up at me in surprise.

"No one taught me, guv'nor," he replied. "I done it like Mr. X."

The very young have the advantage in that they are not analytical. For them it is sufficient to swing the club, leaving the whys and wherefores to their poor misguided elders. This passion for analysis has been the downfall of many fine natural swingers. Not content just to swing the club they must find out how they swing it. They enter the labyrinth of theory, some of them never to emerge. It is a stage through which most good golfers pass. They forsake the naturalness of youth for the inquisitiveness of adolescence. If they survive, and most do, it is a valuable stage in their golfing education. It gives them experience. They emerge from that stage decided in their own mind what are the governing factors which go to make the golf swing. They are more sophisticated, more philosophical, less credulous than they were of the magic properties of pet theories. By trial and error they have found what matters in the golf swing, what makes it at its best a lovely, rhythmic motion.

It is we, the week-end golfers, who are the eternal gropers. We are the gullible public, ever ready to invest our surplus energy in any casual theory, basing all our hopes upon it, working it to death, exaggerating its importance, and finally discarding it in disgust when it proves to be just another South Sea Bubble. The hips, the shoulders, the elbows and the feet all have their part to play, but each must be controlled and allotted its place in the whole. That control lies in the hands whose henchman is the clubhead. The more these two are allied, the better the golf we play. Someone said of the perfect golf swing that it was the poetry of motion. Alas! how often ours is prose cut up into strips!

To keep our hands alive, we must be alive to our hands.

III

SOME AIDS TO LIVE-HANDEDNESS

$\mathcal{B}$y rights this chapter should describe in detail how to obtain this feeling of the clubhead in the hands. It might be expected to reduce the golf swing to sections, and to show in each, what the hands are doing, why they do it, and what effect they have on other members of the body. But I should not be true to my creed if I deviated at this point into the paths of analytical theory. For the golf swing is not a meccano which can be pieced together by screws. I stick to my theme that the secret of better golf is to swing the club with the hands, and to hit the ball with the hands through the medium of the clubhead. Other actions of the body, subsidiary to this control, can be left to look after themselves. It is better to confine the attention to the alliance of the hands and the clubhead. For this combination pays dividends. Yet now I feel I am bound to suggest to the reader some aids for making him more live-handed, and to examine with him certain points in the swing where the hands are in danger of defeat by the body.

After a period without playing, the good golfer finds on re-starting that his hands have become dead. Many have the feeling that their clubs are ounces lighter. The weight of the clubs has not altered, but this lighter feeling is brought about because the hands have lost tone. Lack of exercise has rendered the muscles duller and less sensitive. The clubs feel lighter because the hands cannot sense the clubhead. After a round or two this feeling begins to return, and the revival brings with it a marked improvement in results.

The more we swing the club the more supple and sensitive the hand muscles become, and the quicker that spark is generated from the clubhead to the hands. So the first thing we must do is to tone the hand muscles. I am afraid my past is strewn with the wreckage of many carpets, and therefore I do not advise daily practise on the best Persian at home. A few swings each day in the garden, or on an old mat, are quite sufficient to tone the muscles. If this is impossible, select a club from your bag, grip it in the fingers and then waggle it a few times, striving with each waggle to feel the clubhead.

Some people take great pains. During the war an airman friend of mine had little time for golf and yet he was quite determined to keep in touch with it somehow. So he used to take up with him an ugly, weighted stick which he waggled secretly in his cockpit, no doubt for the sake of his muscles, and perhaps for auld lang syne!

The grips which golfers use are as varied as hybiscus in Ceylon. Many very good players have an unorthodox grip, and I have even seen a scratch player who gripped the club with his hands reversed. Yet although they may vary in type they all obey one principle. They grip the club in the fingers. The most important fingers in each hand are the forefinger and thumb. In an article the other day I saw these forefingers described as the "trigger" fingers. That is to say, in order to grip correctly the forefingers are bent as if for pulling the triggers of

PLATE VI

THE "GALLERY" FINISH

Abe Mitchell has played a No. 5 iron shot to the green. How beautifully easy it seems! He might have just knocked the head off a daisy before playing the real shot. His hands are alive alright. Notice how their absolute control has given to this finish a look of delightful ease.

two pistols, while the thumb rests lightly in each case against the top joint of the forefinger. In this manner the thumb and forefinger of each hand form a V on the shaft of the club. This combination of forefinger and thumb is really the feeler in each hand. As they pinch against the sides of the shaft the presence of the clubhead should become more pronounced. These two fingers in each hand are the manipulative fingers. It is mainly through them that the clubhead is felt. They are the aids to better timing, the key to better golf.

No magic is wrought by the remaining fingers. They function naturally, gripping the club easily and avoiding any tightness or tension. Too tight a grip reduces the feeling in the fingers. Do not be afraid of gripping lightly. The club will not fly out of the hands at the moment of impact, for the natural reaction is to tighten the grip as the clubhead comes to the ball.

The overlapping grip has probably the most followers, and it is certainly the most common among the better players. Since the hands are joined by the overlap of the right little finger on the forefinger of the left, the overlapping grip has the advantage of helping to keep both hands moving in unison. It has come to be regarded as the standard grip in golf.

Having taken the correct grip, the next thing is the stance. It is at this point that so many players lapse into the grotesque. Stand at the first tee of any club on a week-end and you will be able to count on the fingers of one hand the number of players with a natural stance. It must be something psychological, the terror of meeting the ball, which causes so many contortions. The correct way to stand is the way which feels most natural to the player. It is often a matter of build. The taller player will probably have a wider stance. It is more natural for the splay-footed to turn their feet outwards; the reverse will apply to the pigeon-toed. Tension in any form must be avoided, since tenseness at this early stage will remain for the rest of the swing.

It is only a matter of placing the feet comfortably and of inclining the body from the trunk upwards slightly towards the ball. Do not reach out to the ball. Do not stoop. Be comfortable. The knees should be slightly bent with the knee joints relaxed. This will help to give a smooth pivot on the back swing. The ball should lie on a line drawn from just inside the left heel. Since the left hand is above the right on the club, the left shoulder will be uppermost with the right shoulder lower and nearer the ball.

So far we are gripping the club easily in the fingers and feeling the clubhead with those manipulative fingers, the thumb and forefinger of each hand. We are standing naturally, avoiding any tension. If there is no tension, and if we are gripping the club properly, we shall feel the clubhead as we waggle the club in the address. This is its main purpose. A spark has jumped across from the clubhead to the hands. In the address we are cementing the alliance between the clubhead and the hands. We must see to it that nothing comes between them for the remainder of the swing.

The first check point is the beginning of the back swing, and it is here that many players go wrong. So often at this point you see the player raise his shoulders. This is brought about by picking up the club instead of swinging it. By raising the shoulders the player has immediately changed the plane in which the arc of the swing should be described. In order to neutralise this there must be a compensating movement, and it appears in the form of a drop of the shoulders on the downswing.

There is a tendency at this stage to break the wrists, or to take the club back with the left hand only, leaving the right hand to hang loose and lifeless on the shaft. It is true that the left hand must guide, but the right hand must work in unison with it. Therefore, feel for the clubhead with the manipulative fingers of the right hand.

We are going to use BOTH hands at the ball and so we start them back together. If you are PRACTISING this motion try to decapitate an imaginary daisy growing eighteen inches behind the ball. But if you are PLAYING a game, dismiss the daisy from your mind and think only of hitting the ball. The beheading of the imaginary daisy will give the swing a broader arc, thus affording the hands and the clubhead more room to manoeuvre. The break in the wrists will come naturally and the eventual hitting position will be all the stronger if there has been no quick break at the start. I am not going to dwell on the functions of the shoulders and hips, for if the hands are in control their use will develop naturally. It is sufficient to say that these members will pivot over the ball. Do not worry about them, concentrate instead on feeling the clubhead in the hands, and with them guide it to the top of the swing.

The start of the downswing is the second check point. All will be well if the feeling of the clubhead is there, but if it is absent the body will begin to dictate. The result will be that the body will lead the hands and win the race to the ball. The body must be restrained, thus giving the hands and the clubhead the time and space they require for their task. Using the hands as a medium, bring the clubhead smartly through the ball. In other words, hit the ball with the hands.

What happens once the ball is hit does not really matter. It is on its way and nothing we may do can alter its course. But if the hands have really hit the ball, they will carry the clubhead through to what is popularly described as a "gallery" finish. This "gallery" finish is not a special performance enacted for the benefit of press photographers. It is the natural outcome of a swing in which the hands have played the predominant part. It is a feature of all good players, but it can be possessed by anyone who controls the clubhead with the hands.

Watch the first-class professional before he plays each stroke. He selects his club and then stands a pace or two behind his ball, studying the shot he is about to play. All the time he is considering the stroke, his hands are moving and alive. They are flicking the club to and fro in a kind of miniature address. This is not a mannerism but an unconscious effort, the outcome of habit, to feel the clubhead in the hands. It is a brief rehearsal of the performance which is about to begin. The spark is jumping across from the clubhead to the hands.

I have often wondered if it would be sounder to teach the beginner to play the short shots first. It is natural when we begin to crave for a full-blooded blow at the ball. The occasional one we hit stays in our memory for days. Most of us would lack the patience to continue if we were restricted during those agonising initial stages to the bread and water of half-swings. We require a good portion of jam in order to keep our appetite. And yet if we were spartan I feel it would pay handsomely. Begin as you mean to carry on! And if we developed a solid beginning the rest would seem more simple. From the standpoint of control it is easier to lengthen a swing than to reduce it, and it is ironic that in golf the nearer we approach to the hole the harder the game becomes. For reasons too obvious to state, of all the shots in golf the short shots are the most telling. The steepest climb along the road to scratch

PLATE VII

THE SHORT PITCH

A. L. Bentley has played a short pitch to the flag. Short shots should be regarded as drives in miniature, and the same principle holds—control the clubhead with the hands. This principle is well illustrated here. The hands have brought the clubhead crisply through the ball, and together they are following it on its way towards the flag. Note the easy position of the body. No muscle is forced or strained.

lies between that mark and four handicap. These last few strokes are the most difficult of all to discard. As a rule, it is in the short shots that the solution lies. No one can become a good scratch golfer without an effective short game. Rhythm in this department is essential, even more necessary perhaps than in the longer shots. Yet the same principle applies: feel the clubhead and hit the ball crisply with the hands.

It stands to reason that the nearer we are to the hole the less body turn we require. So many handicap players pivot too much, as if relying on the turn of the body and not on a crisp hand action, to send the ball towards the hole. In the short game, more than ever, we must strive to be live-handed. We can afford from the half shots downwards to restrict the body turn, to stay more over the ball, and to let the hands and clubhead do the rest.

And now a word of warning: the easy wristy pitch as played by many good golfers is a pleasantly artistic sight; but it requires a nicety of timing which only natural gifts and years of playing can bring. Such a delicate stroke is too ambitious to be copied by the week-end golfer. For those of us whose play is spasmodic, it is better to use in shots around the green, a little more forearm, a little less wrist. I do not mean by this that the shot should be stiffly played, but mix with a buoyant hand action a pinch of solid forearm. The short shots are best regarded simply as drives in miniature, and the same principle holds. Grip lightly; stand naturally; avoid tension; feel the clubhead in the hands, and mindful always of its purpose, swing it with them crisply through the ball.

I V

MAKING A PLAN

In an earlier chapter I suggested that the ball was brilliantly on the defensive and awaited with confidence the assault of the player. The time the player has for thought is the strong point of this defence. I suggested also that only good generals survive, and I firmly believe this is true. The plan of attack must be sound, based on solid, well-tried principles, and those advocated here are to swing the club with the hands and to hit the ball with them through the medium of the clubhead. First we must think hard and constructively, and then we must act quickly while the plan is fresh in the mind. It is fatal to change the plan half-way through the operation. The result will then be confusion. It is equally disastrous to allow any thoughts of failure to cloud the shape of our object, and we shall not succeed if the mind is focussed on something other than this object. The object, of course, is to hit the ball a certain length in a given direction. It is not our object to turn the left hip, nor to keep the right elbow close to the side on the backswing, since neither manoeuvre, though good in itself, can of its own accord make us hit the ball. Each is only a tactical move in the general plan. Prior to hitting the ball we must first have a clear-cut picture in our mind of the shot we are going to play, and we must retain this picture in our mind of the shot we are going to play, and we must retain this picture throughout the stroke.

Let us consider again the faster games. In lawn tennis we cannot decide the next shot we shall play until the ball is coming at us from the other side of the net. Lawn tennis differs from golf in that our opponent can directly influence our next stroke. As the ball comes over the net we decide at once to play a forehand shot into our opponent's backhand corner. We have at most a couple of seconds in which to make up our mind and play the stroke. Whether the ball pitches on the base line or in the cabbages at the back of the court is quite another matter. The fact is that there is little time in which to dwell on cabbages. The very short interval between the resolve and the completion of the stroke helps us to think constructively, since there is little time for indecision.

It is the same in cricket. The batsman has that very short period from the time the ball leaves the bowler's hand to the playing of the stroke in which to make up his mind. If we are facing someone like Larwood the time is, indeed, very short. Our mind quickly tells us that the stroke required is a drive through the covers, or a glance to leg, and our muscles quickly set about going through the necessary motions. Although in golf our opponent cannot directly influence our stroke, many other things can. Although tennis players need not be cabbage-conscious, most golfers have been in their time acutely aware of woods. Sometimes it has seemed impossible to keep out of them. Bunkers have thrown out their magnetic fields and water has given them a wintry stare. The game of golf was not devised so that a time limit is set for the playing of each stroke. There is room for vacillation. In order to counteract this we must see in our mind the shot successfully played, even before we play it, and as I have already said we must retain this picture of

PLATE VIII

THE FINAL TOUCHES

TO THE PLAN

George Duncan has made his plan, and is adding the final touches to it before he plays the shot. See how the hands are feeling for the clubhead. Before he undertakes the shot his hands will give the club a last flick, and then the vital spark will jump from the clubhead to the hands. Duncan is a great example of a player who makes his plan quickly and carries it through with the minimum delay.

perfection, to the exclusion of everything else, throughout the swing. Having formed a clear picture of how the shot must be played, we must waste no time in playing it. Good bridge players maintain that if tricks must be lost they should be lost quickly. Many of us find this easy whether we play fast or slow. And yet it is good advice. To play quickly has virtue. It suggests decisive thought. Furthermore, it helps to retain in our mind the unblurred picture of the successful shot.

As the ball disappears into a bunker, how often has one heard the remark, "Oh! I knew I should do that." This is an immediate admission that during the stroke the player was thinking of that bunker. He had not filled his mind with the positive picture of the ball carrying successfully over it. How then do we form this picture? Standing on the tee before driving we decide in our mind the point on the fairway at which we wish to play. We then form a picture of the ball flying through the air and landing on the selected spot. This picture we retain until the stroke has been played. It is extraordinary how the muscles will obey the dictates of the mind.

Then again, we may be faced by a long second shot up to the flag with an awkward, unsympathetic wind blowing off the left shoulder. Our first thought is perhaps rather gloomy. We see our ball swinging away to the right and disappearing into deep rough far away from the green. It is better to try and replace such thoughts with the picture of the shot held firmly into the wind, and with this fixed in our mind to set about hitting the ball.

It helps before playing a short pitch, or any stroke around the green, to select the exact spot where we wish the ball to land. Plan the complete shot. See it in the air, see it land on the selected spot with just enough run to take it to the hole. To consider perfection before every stroke may seem to many a conceited and ridiculous practice. Why, they may ask themselves, are they receiving strokes from scratch if they are not among the sinners? It is true we shall fail wholly, or in part, to attain our ideal on many occasions, but we shall fare far worse without a plan which, if it does not unfold to perfection, may well provide us with a thoroughly workable solution. Moreover, the mind is giving the muscles something constructive on which they can set to work.

How many of us, I wonder, play for position? Nearly any two-shot hole has one or more ways in which it should be played. The topography should be studied. From what place on the fairway, we should ask ourselves, do we get the best second shot? Most of us are content to drive straight down the middle without regard to the confirmation of the ground and bunkers around the green. The golf architect, however, is more subtle than we suppose, and unless we study the lie of each hole he will lure us away from the path of true righteousness. To aim from the tee with a driver at a few square yards of fairway may seem an ambitious project for us, the week-end golfers, and yet we are constantly aiming at a green, a target seldom much larger. Greens, too, have their subtleties and the contours of many are so shaped that they suggest to the player either a hook or a slice. These are traps into which we shall surely fall unless we observe them and make such adjustments as are necessary in the playing of the shot.

Some years before this recent war, that great golfer and showman, Walter Hagen, came to the last hole in the Open Championship, at St. Annes, needing a two to tie. The hole itself was over four hundred yards long. After a good drive down the fairway he was faced with a No. 3 iron shot which he knew he must hole. He paused for a moment behind his ball studying the shot, and then, when everyone expected him to select his club and play it, he started to walk forward to the green. Once at the green he made a detailed survey of its contours, deciding where his ball would pitch and how it would run on to the hole. Oblivious of the dense crowd and of the sceptics within it who construed his promenade as nothing more than a piece of showmanship, he returned, quickly chose his club and played the stroke. The happy ending, of course, would be that he holed it. In fact, he just failed to do so, the ball pitching a few inches short of the hole and ending in a bunker at the back of the green. But the moral is there alright. He refused to play that vital shot until he had planned it in detail, caring nothing for the derision which might follow were his plan not wholly successful.

Most of us are not of the moral stature of Hagen, and faced with a similar predicament in the monthly bogey, we should not like to run the risk of the mild ridicule which would follow were we seen with our ball on the fairway, two hundred yards behind us. But who is to know it if we have a clear picture of the shot in our mind, sharpened even to the point of seeing it disappear into the hole? At any rate, we could seek comfort inside the clubhouse, knowing that although we failed, we knew what we had to do and how we proposed to do it.

V

JUSTIFICATION

When a humble amateur, and a week-end golfer at that, writes a book on the game it is reasonable to ask him to state his justification. He must explain his confounded cheek. My justification may be slender, but it is two-fold. Golf has formed a part of my life for the last thirty years, and to it I owe a very great deal. It is difficult to be connected with anything for so long without forming in that time certain fixed ideas. I have admitted in an earlier chapter that when I had the time I studied the game and made experiments, and I am open to the accusation that I allocated more time to golf and less to other and more important things, than I should have done in those days. But I do not regret it. It was fun. And if I partially neglected certain aspects of History, I think I learned something about golf. Besides, a modest connection with the game has given me opportunities to study at close quarters the methods of many of its best players, to discuss this elusive game with them, and even to play against some. So much for my first justification.

As I ploughed my crooked furrow through the tempting soil of theory, I was often conscious of the feeling of surfeit, of having too much of a good thing. Yet each field seemed more fertile than the last and I could not resist the temptation to plough through it. It might have continued like that and one might have died a ploughman. I realised at last, that the only thing to do was to stand aside and review the entire cultivation. What field or what area produced the richest crop? For there would be found the soil that was most worth while. I decided then, and I have seen no reason to change, that the basis of the game of golf was the alliance between the hands and the clubhead: the closer and the more sensitive the alliance of these two the better the player. It is this alliance which enables the good golfer to produce the shot again and again with an almost monotonous precision. It accounts for his excellent ball control, that ability to string the shots together and to place them where he wishes them to go. It is the temporary rift in this alliance which causes us to score our sevens and eights after playing a few preceding holes in, or near, par figures. It may explain the light and shade of a lawn tennis player I once knew, who, in a qualifying round of a tournament, went out in 54 and came home in 32!

However light-hearted a player may be, and golf was meant to be enjoyed, he is a liar if he denies that he wishes to play as well as his limitations will allow. Yet I believe it is a fact that nine out of every ten week-end golfers are not making the most of the golf that is in them. I feel they are not doing so, because their game is not based on any sound formula, a formula known to the player, to which he will turn when playing badly, and on which he can then rebuild his game. Even with the best, the game of golf turns in cycles. There is the crescendo to the peak of form. There is that glorious light-headed and dizzy period when we reach and remain at the peak, so confident as a rule, that we think of nothing but hitting the ball and hitting it as hard as we can. According to our ability, there follows either a crash or a gradual slither downwards from the champagne heights of success. This is the time when our game should receive an overhaul, a time when we should return to first principles to see if they are being neglected. But first we must decide what these principles are. We must base our game on something.

Many handicap players express surprise when it is suggested to them that they are completely dead-handed; that they are not swinging the clubhead with the hands; and that the only limbs in direct contact with the club are being left far behind in the mad rush with the body to get at the ball. Either completely baffled, or obsessed with the importance of some movement in the swing, and exaggerating its importance in consequence, they struggle on hoping that things will come right. A sound formula is lacking to help them regain their game.

I believe that by thinking only of his hands, by swinging the club with them, and by hitting the ball with the hands, through the medium of the clubhead, the long handicap golfer can take strokes off his game. I believe this since I have seen it happen frequently. I have seen players in the course of a round find a golf swing they never possessed before. Their movements, previously stilted and laboured, have suddenly become natural and have fitted smoothly into place. They did so, firstly, because the swing was properly controlled, and secondly, because these movements were not studied. The player's energy was redirected to the only object of the golf swing, namely to hit the ball. His game gained in control since he was swinging the clubhead with the hands, conscious of it throughout the swing, and bringing it to the ball with the only part of his anatomy capable of the task, that is to say, the hands. I believe, also, that if we are playing badly, attention to this formula will do more than anything to revive in us this feeling, the feeling of something to hit with, without which we cannot play golf.

The close relationship between the hands and the clubhead is not an innovation, The best swings have honoured it since golf began. It has been recognised by the best players of recent years. But in playing with friends in the higher handicap grades, I formed the notion that it was not as widely recognised as it might have been.

There is an old proverb which says: "He that bewaileth himself hath the cure in his hands."

And that is my second justification.